LUNAR BASES

LUNAR BASES

SHAARON COSNER

FRANKLIN WATTS • A FIRST BOOK • 1990
NEW YORK • LONDON • TORONTO • SYDNEY

Cover photograph courtesy of NASA

All photographs courtesy of NASA

Library of Congress Cataloging-in-Publication Data

Cosner, Shaaron.
Lunar bases / by Shaaron Cosner.
p.   cm.—(A First book)
Includes bibliographical references.
Summmary: Discusses recent proposals for colonizing the moon,
adjustments necessary to support human life, and conditions which
settlers might encounter.
ISBN 0-531-10894-5
1. Lunar bases—Juvenile literature. [1. Lunar bases. 2. Moon—
Exploration.] I. Title. II. Series.
TL799.M6C67   1990
919.9'104—dc20   89-22729   CIP   AC

CONTENTS

Chapter One
The Explorers 9

Chapter Two
The New Frontier 23

Chapter Three
The Pioneers 34

Chapter Four
The Builders 44

Chapter Five
The Prospectors 50

Glossary 59
For Further Reading 61
Index 62

LUNAR BASES

The year is 2010. The company you are working for has just assigned you to be one of this country's next explorers. The area you will be exploring is located on the moon.

Preparing for the 238,857-mile (384,404 km) journey to the moon is a simple task in the year 2010. You just have to make sure you are physically fit, and perhaps lose a few pounds. You will not be allowed on board the space vehicles to the moon unless you are in tip-top condition and have a doctor's release saying you have no diseases or physical disabilities. Other than that, almost anyone can go to the moon.

Your company will probably provide you with the special clothes you need. All you will have to do is get someone to watch the dog and to water the plants while you are gone. In no time at all, you will be on your way to the Kennedy Space Center for your trip.

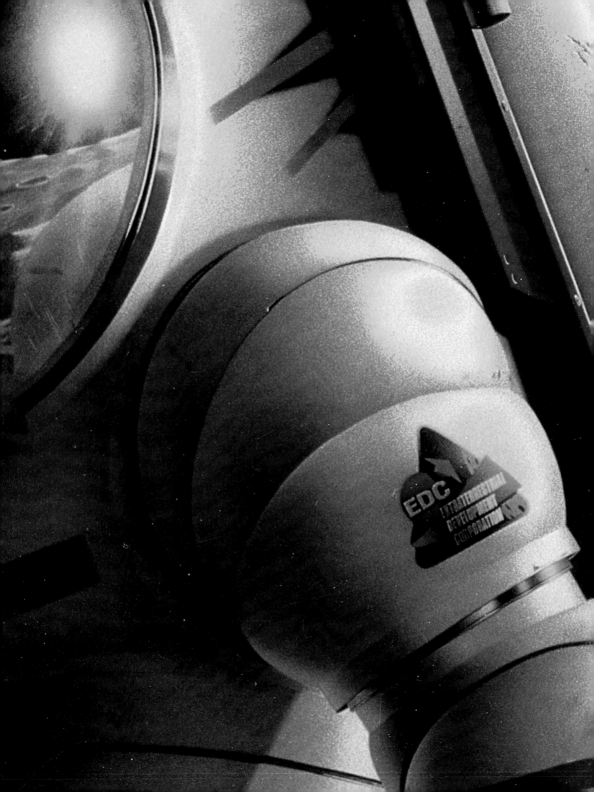

An evolutionary approach to settling the inner solar system would begin with an outpost on the moon. The explorer in the foreground wears a space suit with rotating joints. A lunar oxygen-production plant, to the right of a large solar panel, is generating a supply of rocket fuel that will eventually be used for a trip to Mars.

The Space Center will be filled with people coming and going, much like our airports are now. You join other passengers in the lounge to wait for your flight. Your baggage has been carefully weighed because the space shuttles can only carry so much weight.

Finally, your flight is announced over the loudspeaker. A bus takes you to the launching pad. You strap yourself in your seat. Your heart begins to beat more rapidly as the giant engines fire up and the ship begins to vibrate. You view the launch on a video screen. Suddenly, you realize the Earth is getting smaller. You are on your way to the moon.

During the trip to the moon, you will be able to get out of your seat and practice walking in *zero gravity*. There are walkways overhead so you can hold on to rails until you get over the weird feelings zero gravity causes. You will also learn how to eat and drink, relax in a chair, and use the toilet in a weightless environment.

Soon the *cargo bay* doors open and you can see thousands of miles of space as well as your old planet, Earth, below. The sky has changed from blue to black when you approach your first stop, a space station. After *docking*, you wait in another lounge for your *lunar* spaceship, which is running late. Some things never change.

Eventually, your lunar spaceship flight is ready and you make your way to your seat. The spaceship blasts off. About eight hours later, you see the lunar surface. The spaceship lands, and you walk to the elevator that will take you down to the moon's surface and your new job at the lunar base.

Such an adventure may seem like something out of a science-fiction movie, but there is a very good chance that

The lunar ferry, at center, will also take people
to the moon. In left center background is a space
station facility as envisioned by some NASA
planners. In lower left corner is propellant dump,
which houses the liquid hydrogen tank modules
needed for the trip to the moon. At right bottom
is a free-floating shuttle external tank.

you could be working on or visiting the moon by the year 2010. Already companies and corporations are offering trips into space. One company, Society Expeditions, has 121 people signed up, each of whom paid a $5,000 deposit for the trip! The trip itself will probably cost over a million dollars. Still, by the year 2025, it is estimated there will be 100,000 tourists flying the friendly skies of space.

Aside from everyday tourists willing to pay a million or so dollars to travel in space, who would be interested in setting up a lunar base? The Japanese are interested. Japan is preparing a lunar mission for 1990 that will allow it to make future flights to the moon and eventually, other planets, in Muses-A, its spacecraft. The Soviet Union has a manned lunar vehicle and a team of *cosmonauts* ready to travel to the moon. The United States has planned for years to establish a lunar base on the moon. In April 1986, the National Commission on Space presented its program for human settlements on the moon by 2017 and on Mars by 2027. The Commission called its report, "Pioneering the Space Frontier, Our Next 50 Years in Space" and dedicated it to the crew of the *Challenger*.

What a future lunar landing facility might look like. The pressurized vehicle in the foreground is connected to the lander by a transfer tunnel. This allows the crew easy access. Earth appears over the mountains at right.

Before people can go to the moon, they will need three new transporters: a *low-orbit* cargo vehicle, a passenger vehicle perhaps smaller than the space shuttles today for travel to and from *low Earth orbit,* and a "workhorse" transfer ship to carry both people and cargo. More advanced rockets will also be needed to get these vehicles into space. We will

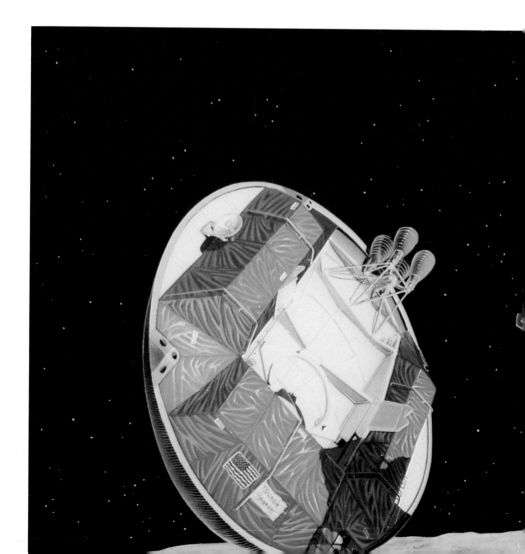

need engines that can be run from raw materials mined from *asteroids*, the moon, and the Martian moons of Phobos and Deimos.

Before humans are sent to live on the moon, *robots* will probably build factories there to handle all the materials scientists expect to find.

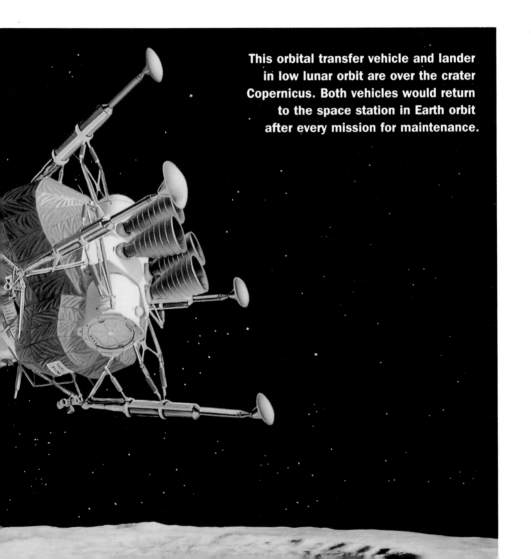

This orbital transfer vehicle and lander in low lunar orbit are over the crater Copernicus. Both vehicles would return to the space station in Earth orbit after every mission for maintenance.

There are many problems to be solved, and it will cost an enormous amount of money to put people on the moon. So why bother? For one thing, scientists say, a moon base will allow astronomers to observe the sun and even distant universes from the moon with giant *observatories*. These giants will produce really clear images because they won't be affected by things like light pollution and television and telephone signals like they are on the Earth.

Giant astronomy *satellites* planned for the moon could be repaired by engineers living on the lunar base. Scientific instruments, star-trackers, and radio antennas could be repaired, too. This would save millions of dollars a year because the telescopes or broken parts would not have to be returned to Earth every time they needed to be fixed. The space telescopes could go about the business of providing information about *black holes* in space and locating *anti-matter* in the universe.

In past years, space shuttle astronauts have saved the United States thousands of dollars by repairing satellites in space. What if engineers living on the moon could keep the many satellites cruising in space in top working order? In something that looks like a scene from *2001: A Space Odyssey,* huge repair ships with repair crews would slide up to the satellite, hook it to the repair ship, and tow it to the moon to be fixed. Communications satellites cost about $100 million apiece right now. There are over a hundred in orbit. Think of the savings if they could be repaired in space!

Experiments on the moon will result in some wonderful products to make life on Earth easier. Powerful networks will offer hundreds of new ways for humans to communicate

Astronauts break ground for the installation of a new telescope for an observatory on the far side of the moon.

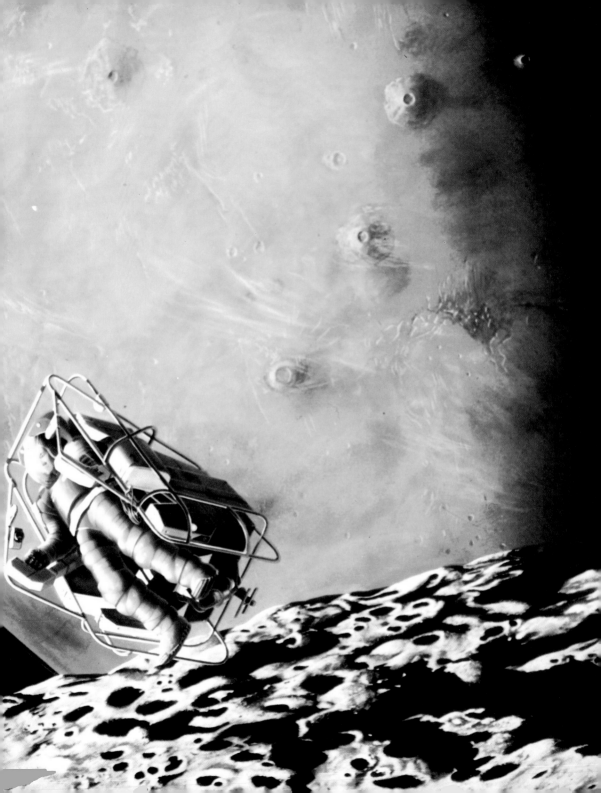

Colonization of the moon could lead to expeditions to other planets. In this illustration, two astronauts explore the surface of Phobos, a moon of Mars. Mars, as it would appear to the human eye from Phobos, looms on the horizon. The explorers have descended in a small "excursion" vehicle, and they are navigating with the aid of a personal spacecraft.

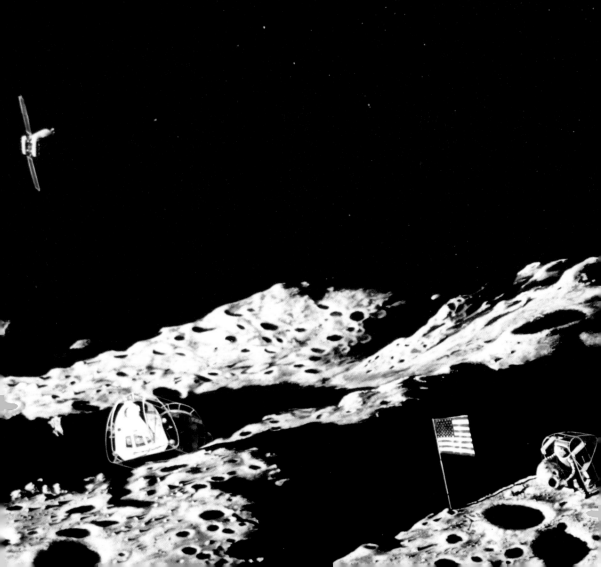

with each other. Radiophones, navigation sets, and emergency-rescue systems will be worn like wristwatches. Traffic-control systems will be super-efficient. Burglar detectors will cut down on crime. Fire detectors and fault locators that can predict earthquakes will make life safer on Earth.

The population of the Earth is doubling every thirty-five years. What will happen if there is no more room on Earth? Scientists believe the moon might be used to hold thousands of people. Some scientists are looking even farther than the moon for future colonization.

The exploration and colonization of the moon is as exciting today as when the first frontier settlers went out to explore Earth. It will allow the children of today, when they are adults, to go way beyond the limits of the space we know. As far as many scientists are concerned, all systems are go for a lunar base on the moon.

TWO   THE NEW FRONTIER

What will the environment on the moon be like for the new lunar bases? Like the early pioneers on Earth, early moon pioneers will have to get used to wide-open spaces. The great plains of the moon, called seas by Galileo, the great sixteenth-century astronomer, stretch for miles. Huge mountains, 1,000 to 20,000 feet (300 to 6,100 m) high, will easily be conquered because humans will be weightless on the moon. Huge craters, some 5 to 100 miles (8 to 160 km) in diameter, dot the moon. (On Earth craters are no more than 6 to 7 miles—9.7 to 11.3 km—in diameter.)

Not a single sign of life will be seen away from the lunar base because the moon is a "dead world." There is no air or other atmosphere—no clouds, no winds, no rain, no snow. People on the moon will never have to worry about rain ruining their picnics or sporting events. They will never

worry about the wind toppling over their structures. The only noise the pioneers will hear will be the voices of other lunar workers transmitted through their helmets.

Scientists have already been able to analyze some of the moon rocks brought back from other space missions. They have found that the moon is covered with two types of

Although the moon does not look like a very welcoming place, scientists and others believe we can learn an enormous amount from this distant place by traveling there.

rocks. One kind looks like it came from volcanoes; the other type is made up of many materials mixed together.

Lunar rocks can be very hot because they are exposed to the sun fourteen days at a time. Only one-tenth of the moon's heat is reflected; nine-tenths is absorbed by the surface. Temperatures range from 200 degrees below to 200 degrees above zero Fahrenheit (about $-130°C$ to $+90°C$) so the rocks cool rapidly when the lunar "night" comes around.

Scientists are working on providing what they call a "shirtsleeve environment" on the moon. That means they will try to make the moon as earthlike as possible. In the airless atmosphere of the moon, oxygen will have to be manufactured. Scientists hope to extract oxygen from rocks and mountains on the moon. They also think some oxygen can be manufactured by plants and vegetables like pumpkins that yield large amounts of oxygen. Pumpkins also soak up carbon dioxide that is exhaled. Eventually, it is hoped such plants and vegetables can be grown on the moon, but until they are, they will be brought to the space-station cargo dock by cargo rockets.

Humans can survive on pure oxygen, but they also need nitrogen and helium for their *metabolism*. (Pure oxygen is a fire hazard too.) Nitrogen and helium will also have to be obtained, and scientists hope to find hydrogen on the moon. If they do not find hydrogen, they will import it from Earth. The hydrogen will also be "mixed" with oxygen to make water, unless scientists can use ice trapped in the shadowy areas near the moon's poles. Then a colony would probably be built near one of the poles so colonists would always have water.

The same full-time, intense sunlight that hits the moon may be the main source of energy for lunar pioneers. Solar-powered satellites would deliver energy to the people. Receivers would be located near where the energy is needed. In fact, there is enough space around the moon for hundreds of solar-powered satellites.

This artist's concept of lunar mining operations
illustrates the production of liquid oxygen. At center
a robot front loader scoops up lunar soil, which is then
dumped into sifters. From there, a complicated process
follows that finally results in liquid oxygen. Workers
would be housed in the tall structure at top center.

An outpost on the lunar surface with space
nuclear power units in the background.

For those days when there is no sun, scientists are experimenting with storing up sunlight, using batteries or spinning *flywheels* that would rotate at high speeds during periods of sunshine. They have considered using nuclear reactors, but worry about getting rid of the dangerous wastes. They are not worried about nuclear accidents, on the other hand, because there would be no atmosphere to spread a *fallout* up on the moon.

Scientists might decide to go with solar panels at first, and maybe add nuclear stations as they advance to bigger and bigger colonies. Whatever they decide to do, control of the temperatures will allow the residents to decide their climate, their seasons, and their weather.

Probably the biggest adjustment humans will have to make in their new environment on the moon is living in a weightless environment. Scientists in the United States, France, and the Soviet Union already have volunteers who spend anywhere from one week to one year undergoing experiments in weightlessness. These volunteers lie in bed at a 6-degree slant with their feet higher than their heads. This is the closest scientists could come to *simulating* the effects of weightlessness here on Earth. The volunteers eat by propping themselves up on one elbow. They shower in bed using a hand-held nozzle. They use bedpans instead of toilets, and they exercise by moving their legs in the air or by doing *isometrics*.

Scientists are worried about the effects of weightlessness on the moon because they already know some things that can happen to people. For one thing, they know the body starts to get rid of fluids right away. This is because when there is no *gravity,* the blood and other body fluids drift to the upper parts of the body. The brain thinks the whole body is overloaded with fluids and starts trying to get rid of them by sweating or urinating.

The minute the body enters a weightless environment, the heart pumps less blood and has to beat faster to keep up. The muscles, with no gravity to resist, begin to atrophy, or waste away. The bones start to lose calcium almost immediately and the calcium goes to the blood. When calcium gets into the blood, it can cause painful kidney stones within hours. The immune system also changes slightly, which means people may get illnesses and diseases more quickly.

Space travelers may also suffer from motion sickness for up to four days at the beginning of their journey and when they land on the moon. Motion sickness may cause a person to be lazy and irritable. He or she may have headaches and vomit. Perhaps the pioneers will have to do what the Soviet cosmonauts do after long space voyages. They slide down a special chute from their capsule and are carried around in a sedan chair for days or weeks until they get used to the Earth's gravity once more.

Being weightless on the moon would be a tremendous adjustment for people to make. This artist's concept of an astronaut's room on board a permanently manned space station illustrates weightlessness.

The only other way to find out how a weightless environment will affect the lunar-base astronauts is to actually put people in space for long periods of time. In November 1988, Soviet cosmonauts circled the globe 330 times in the space station *Mir*. The two cosmonauts on board the station broke the space endurance record of 326 days. It is hoped that their voyage and the work of the volunteers on Earth will lead to special diets, fluid control, and new gravity suits so people can survive the harsh environment of the moon.

Putting people in space often and for long periods of time would enable scientists to study the long-term effects of space travel. This artist's concept shows a transportation depot in Mars orbit.

THREE

THE PIONEERS

Living in the alien environment found on the moon is going to be rough, but scientists and engineers are working hard to make life easier for the moon pioneers. One of the most important problems to be solved will be real estate. Just as the pioneers on Earth had to build and design their own houses, engineers are working on moon homes.

At first engineers thought the astronauts could live in the vehicle that took them to the moon, but this idea was quickly discarded. The vehicle might be damaged by *meteorite* hits or radiation. Also, like a car, if the vehicle sat idle too long, it might not start when the astronauts wanted to return to Earth. Instead, engineers decided a special shelter would be necessary. That would leave the vehicle free to travel back and forth as it should.

Engineers have already come up with a number of simple designs to house people on the moon. Most planners agree the first houses on the moon should include one living and dining module called the "habitat." There might also be one or two interconnected laboratories, a factory, a storage center, a garage where the space vehicles will dock, and solar panels to provide power.

Some designs for lunar houses were presented to NASA (National Aeronautics and Space Administration) as long ago as 1964. One proposal said houses should be prefabricated—built ahead of time. Sections would be sent to the moon in cargo rockets. There would be a main shelter unit, and each year a room would be added.

Habitation pods would be made of a flexible material so they could be folded and packed inside the vehicle. Scientists are testing a material called Kenlar, which is as thin as paper and very strong, strong enough to protect the inhabitants from micrometeoroids. This material is already being used on Earth for sails on boats and bulletproof vests.

Since moon inhabitants will be constantly bombarded with *atoms*, scientists are considering putting a plastic layer of aluminum over the exteriors of the houses. Also being tested is a self-sealing "skin" invented years ago. This skin is self-sealing because it is made of little plastic balls. If the material is punctured, air escaping from the pressurized compartment would melt the balls and fill up the hole.

Private researchers have come up with the idea that, with no processing at all, lunar materials can provide a shield against *cosmic rays* for living and working quarters. Using

Left: Future pioneers will travel across the lunar surface to determine, among other things, the best places to build lunar housing. Above: This painting shows a surface-exploration crew investigating a small lava tunnel to determine if it could be used as a natural shelter for the habitation module of a lunar base.

lunar soil brought back by the astronauts, scientists have learned to make the soil into a strong, tough, building material.

Some engineers have suggested building lunar homes partially underground or perhaps into the side of a mountain. The houses would be connected by passageways, corridors, and underground tunnels. They would be divided by fire walls and airtight compartments. People and supplies would enter through an air lock. Some air would be lost, just as some water enters submarines when the hatches are opened, but the oxygen would be quickly replaced.

Another way to make space pioneers more comfortable would be to design homes that countered the effects of low gravity. Gravity would be artificially produced on the moon by attaching two small crew compartments to each other by a cable and rotating one around the other. Experiments would tell us how much rotation would be needed to keep people comfortable.

Designers are also trying to decide how to connect the modules. Perhaps they will be arranged in giant circles or strung together like caterpillars. Another suggestion has been to build "spacehabs" composed of two to eight mushroom-shaped pods.

One of the largest designs for a living space ever discussed would measure 3,288 feet long (1 kilometer) and 656 feet in diameter (200 meters). It would revolve once every twenty-one seconds and hold 10,000 people. It would weigh about 520,000 metric tons, including 20,000 tons of aluminum and 10,000 tons of glass. It would carry 50,000 tons of water and a 1,000-ton generator plant; 420,000 tons of soil, rock, and construction materials; 5,400 tons of liquid hydrogen; and 2,000 tons of people and their belongings.

One of the smaller designs being discussed is to construct the space station from the space shuttles' external fuel tanks. This would be very economical since the tanks are destroyed anyway. The external tanks could be divided into living space for a three-person crew. The shuttle would dock, still carrying its external tank. Solar panels would be attached and connected. The propellants would be cleaned out of the external tank and then the tank would be pressurized. If the astronauts needed more room, more external tanks could be added.

Whatever the design, the moon base and possibly the space stations would eventually be like miniature villages, complete with landscaping, air, water, sunlight, day-and-night cycles, and even seasons. They might eventually be as tall as the World Trade Center in New York City and as wide as Manhattan. They might be so heavy they would be unable to support their own weight without collapsing if they were on Earth. But on the moon, where the gravity is low, the sky's the limit.

After designing a living space, the next most important problem is providing food for the pioneers on the moon. Only a limited amount of fresh food will be able to be flown to the moon, so people will have to set aside areas for growing fresh vegetables and fruits. Experiments are being conducted both on Earth and in space shuttles to find out which will survive. NASA is also working to develop an eatable *algae* that can be grown in space, but they feel it will be important for morale that space people have "real" food rather than something like "nutrition pills" or the freeze-dried food that can be mixed with water.

Only the healthiest people will be picked to go to the moon, but when someone does get sick, everything will be ready. Researchers are working on a health care center that would be computer-run. It would diagnose illness or injuries, and doctors on Earth would prescribe the actual treatment of the moon patient. The treatment would be given by an astronaut "paramedic" and, of course, eventually there would be a whole staff of doctors and nurses stationed on the moon. A moon health station is essential because it might take up to twenty-one days for a rescue spaceship to arrive. This spaceship would cost $100 to $500 million to launch, with no guarantee that the patient would still be alive when it got there.

To perform surgery on someone living on the moon, special surgical tools will have to be designed because of the low gravity. For instance, if the surgeon had to perform abdominal surgery, the patient's bowels would rise up out of the belly unless special retractors or clamps were used to hold them down. Special precautions will have to be made for keeping moon hospitals sterile. On Earth, contamination travels downward. In space and on the moon, doctors will

This is a design for an emergency rescue vehicle. This particular one would be based at a space station.

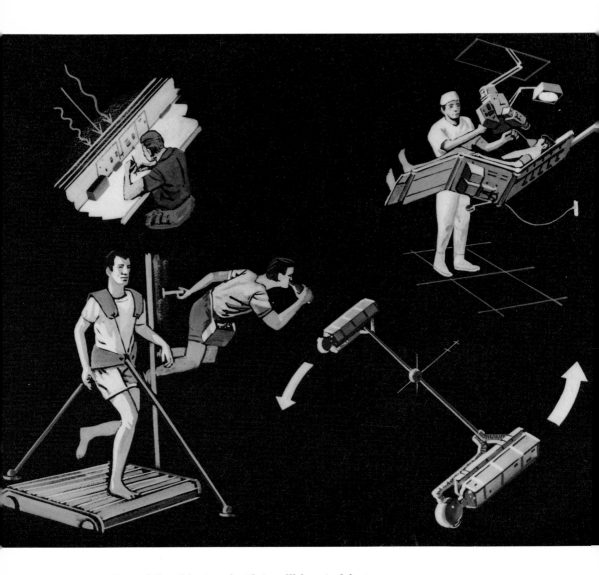

One of the things scientists will be studying as people begin to travel to the moon is the effect the moon's environment will have on exercise.

have to find out which way contamination travels so that area will be the one kept sterile.

Because of the low-gravity effects, exercise will be important for people on the moon. Space stations and lunar bases will probably have some kind of exercise facilities with treadmills and stationary bicycles and rowboats. Doctors will oversee a strict exercise program. It is hoped that the mind will be exercised, too, with books, concerts, and perhaps even television.

Although things may be primitive on the moon at first, as they once were in the cities on Earth, the inhabitants will know that eventually civilization will come to their planet.

FOUR   THE BUILDERS

Just as our nation was built by a variety of people from a variety of countries, the lunar base will eventually be populated with hundreds of people from all walks of life. Scientists from all nations will be conducting studies under conditions of a perfect vacuum. Medical researchers will study the effects of gravity on the human body and other health problems. *Seismologists* will study quake activity on the moon so they can learn more about quakes on Earth. *Meteorologists* will study the weather and be able to predict it worldwide. Nutrition and agricultural experts will study ways to grow living plants on the moon, and *geologists* will study the moon's interior, surface, and mountains. Perhaps they will find the answer to the mystery of the creation of the universe.

of the moon will be populated with all kinds of people doing many different things. A roving vehicle similar to the one used on three Apollo missions is depicted in the foreground.

Firemen, plumbers, welders, air-conditioning experts, mechanics, and electricians will be busy repairing breakdowns and making sure the backup equipment is in good order. They will be constantly on alert to repair punctures made by bombardments of particles in space.

None of this can take place, however, until the construction workers and engineers have begun their work. They will begin with a series of lunar expeditions to follow up those already done by the robots. On the expeditions, they will plan routes across the wide stretches of lunar landscapes and decide on the best areas in which to place habitat modules.

The next chore for moon workers will be construction of the lunar bases, solar-powered satellites, and space-based antennas. They would be involved in four major steps in space construction—making beams to build the structures, assembling the beams in space, getting them into place on the moon, and putting together their final product. Engineers estimate a huge structure a mile (1.6 km) long could be assembled in less than a day.

Equipment will be arriving in a steady stream. It will first be sent to a point in low-Earth orbit. Then it will be transferred to a space tug capable of carrying several shuttle-loads of gear. These space tugs are known as the workhorses of space. Shaped like large cylindrical vans with spidery legs, they will be used to carry equipment and people into orbit around the moon. Then the tugs will be met by another type of transporter that will carry the cargo to the moon's surface.

At first some of the structures might be built on Earth, and then taken apart and the individual sections transported by spacecraft to assembly areas on the moon. They might be unloaded in space where they would float around tethered together until they were ready to be used.

Many of the structures can be assembled in space. Construction crews will buzz around with their jetpacks on their backs wearing special space suits and accessories. They will have to spend many hours practicing before they begin work because the spacesuits severely limit movement, especially the use of fingers and hands. One researcher says it's like working with five or six pairs of heavy gloves and five or six overcoats on. Another says it's like trying to sew while wearing a baseball mitt. Once they have mastered their equipment, they will be able to move huge structures with one hand because of the weightlessness. The sections might look like giant Tinker Toys as more and more girders are added, but they will always be lightweight.

Not all projects will be constructed by human workers. Some will still be controlled by electromechanical manipulators like some of their robot pioneers. A 300-foot (91.4-m) antenna has already been designed, for instance, that can be collapsed and stored in the cargo bays. Once in orbit, the antenna's mechanism would be triggered by the people aboard the spaceship. The huge "dish" would unfold by itself and would be working in an hour.

Remote manipulator arms will also handle beams and retrieve spacecraft from the cargo ships that transport goods to the moon. Flexible joints like human shoulders, elbows,

and wrists will enable these arms to free humans from many everyday tasks like assembling beams.

The tools that the construction workers bring with them will probably be new. (Almost everything in the moon program has had to be invented. These inventions have resulted in other technology such as pocket calculators, laser disks, and cable television.) Perhaps the workers will tether the new tools to their bodies to keep them from drifting off in space. Then they can pound, hammer, and weld the huge structure together—all in the silence of space.

Remote manipulator arms will be used for a variety of tasks in space. This Flight Telerobotic Servicer assembles sections of the permanently manned space station's structure in this artist's conception.

FIVE   THE PROSPECTORS

Prospectors will explore the moon just as prospectors on Earth once searched for the minerals and metals that would make their nations rich. This will become very important if the mineral sources on Earth continue to disappear. Scientists believe there is a very good chance that some of the same minerals and metals found on Earth might be found in the solar system. If prospectors were successful on the moon, eventually they could mine other planets and asteroids. And it would be cheaper since it takes less than 5 percent as much energy to lift them in space as it does on Earth.

Prospectors on the moon will use bulldozers to dig up the ground. Conveyors will take the materials to plants where they will be processed into compact form for shipment.

This painting depicts two scientists of an ice-prospecting lunar mission examining an ice-encrusted drill. Scientists believe that the discovery of ice on the moon would enhance the ability to develop a self-sustaining lunar colony.

An artist's conception of a lunar supply base. Lunar soil contains many elements that provide the basis for industry and life on earth. One possible approach to developing industry in space is to use moon soil as a source of raw materials.

Unlike construction equipment, much of the mining equipment will be the same as that used in the coalfields back on Earth. In fact, this equipment may be even more efficient on the moon because there is no vegetation to worry about. Miners won't have to worry about the environment. The moon is already pockmarked.

The soil will be gathered and processed. (Robots may be able to process 150 tons of raw lunar ore in one month!) Once the soil is processed, it would be catapulted into space at regular intervals by a machine called a mass driver.

The track of the mass driver will look like a racetrack with small buckets hurtling along, one at a time. Coils will generate strong magnetic forces that will increase the speeds of each payload carrier as it passes by, one every two seconds. It will be kept at just the right speed because laser beams would signal when the speed was just a fraction of an inch off. A computer will correct the speed.

The payloads will climb away from the moon to a collection point deep in space. The carrier will release its payload, slow down, and make its return trip to the moon to pick up more materials.

Once the payload is catapulted into space, it will drift to a point thousands of miles behind the moon. It will be caught by a gigantic metallic screen called a "catcher's mitt." When the mitt is filled up, the cargo will be dumped into a storage bin until an ore carrier arrives to take it away to a space-colony processing center. There, solar-powered melters will break down the ore into such products as aluminum, silicon, and oxygen.

Some of the lunar soil won't be processed. It will be used in 6-foot-thick (1.8 m) walls to provide protection from cosmic rays or other bombardments in space. It will cover the human habitat modules and laboratories to protect people from solar flares and potential military threats. Bunkers may also be built to protect the space stations from laser damage in a *Star Wars* type of attack. Scientists already believe they may have the ideal site for the mass drivers—the Descartes highlands, found by astronauts John Young and Charles Drake during the *Apollo 16* mission in 1972.

Scientists estimate that eventually miners will handle thousands of tons of lunar materials each year, using machinery built on the moon. The mining process could produce more than 90 percent of the materials required for building and living on the moon. The moon would no longer be a hostile environment for people. It would be self-sufficient.

Not everyone likes the idea of putting a lunar base or manned space station into space. Some people think that the billions of dollars used to carry out such a scheme would buy a lot of equipment back on Earth. Some feel that hurrying to complete such a project would be like a large corporation spending billions of dollars building a plant before they had the technology to deal with it.

Even some scientists oppose the project. James Van Allen, a famous scientist who discovered radiation belts around the Earth, called the projects for the space stations "busywork." Other scientists feel the project will take money away from scientific projects on Earth.

The moon is the nearest source of resources other than the
Earth itself. Research from the Apollo program revealed
that the moon is rich in many elements. Shown here is an
artist's illustration of a lunar operation.

Despite the criticism, the project is going ahead. If all goes well, construction will begin soon and by the turn of the century, the lunar colony may have been started. A new frontier will be waiting for those explorers, colonists, prospectors, miners, and industrialists who want to tame it. A new frontier will be waiting for you!

GLOSSARY

Algae: A group of very simple plants

Antimatter: Matter in which the electrical charges are the opposite of those in matter that makes up all physical objects

Asteroids: Any of several hundred small planets between Mars and Jupiter

Atoms: The smallest pieces of matter that make up everything in the universe

Black Hole: A space formed by the death of a star

Cargo Bay: An area in spaceships used for storing goods and/or merchandise

Cosmic Rays: Harmful beams of light radiated from stars, including the sun

Cosmonaut: A Russian astronaut

Docking: The act of connecting two objects, usually space vehicles, to one another

Fallout: The falling to Earth of matter after the explosion of an atomic bomb

Flywheel: A wheel heavy enough to resist sudden changes in speed that can damage working parts in a machine

Geologist: One who studies the Earth's rocks to learn about its structure and history

Gravity: The invisible force of attraction that gives an object its weight or heaviness

Isometrics: Equal in measurement

Low Earth Orbit: The path of a satellite around the Earth that travels 125 miles above the Earth's atmosphere

Lunar: Dealing with or related to the moon

Metabolism: The chemical processes constantly taking place in a living organism

Meteorite: A solid particle from space that hits the Earth in one or more pieces

Meteorologist: One who studies the atmosphere or weather and makes predictions based on those studies

Observatory: A building used for viewing and studying the skies

Propellants: An agent that causes something to be driven forward in motion

Robot: Any machine that operates automatically or is remote controlled

Satellite: An object made by people that orbits a heavenly body

Seismologist: One who studies earthquakes

Simulate: To mimic, imitate, or to appear or sound like

Zero Gravity: Weightlessness; absence of gravity

FOR FURTHER READING

Ardley, Neil. *Out into Space*. New York: Franklin Watts, 1981.

Branley, Franklyn M. *Space Colony*. New York: Elsevier Nelson, 1982.

Ciupik, Larry A. *Space Machines.* Milwaukee: Raintree Childrens Books, 1979.

DiCerto, Joseph J. *Star Voyages*. New York: Messner, 1981.

Fradin, Dennis B. *Space Colonies*. Chicago: Childrens Press, 1985.

Smolders, P.L.L. *Living in Space: A Handbook for Space Travelers*. Blue Ridge Summit, Pa.: Tab Books, 1986.

Trefil, James S. *Living in Space*. New York: Scribner, 1981.

INDEX

Algae, eatable, 39
Aluminum, 35, 54
Antennas, space-based, 46, 47
Anti-matter, 18
Apollo 16, 55
Astronomy satellites, 18
Atoms, 35

Black holes, 18
Bunkers, 55

Carbon dioxide, 26
Cargo bay, 12
"Catcher's mitt," 54
Challenger, 15
Construction equipment, 49
Cosmic rays, 35
    protection from, 55

Cosmonauts, 15, 30, 33
Craters, 23

Delmos, 17
Descartes highlands, 55
Docking, 12
Drake, Charles, 55

Engineers, 18, 34, 35
Exercise program, 42, 43

Fallout, 29
Flywheels, 29
Food, 39–40
Fuel tanks, external, constructing
    living space from, 39

Galileo, 23

Geologists, 44
Gravity:
    artificially produced, 38
    low-gravity effects, 30
    zero, 12

Habitat, 35
Habitation pods, 35
Health-care center, 40, 43
Helium, 26
Housing. See Lunar houses
Hydrogen, 26

Ice, 26, 51
Isometrics, 29

Japan, lunar mission of, 15

Kenlar, 35

Lasers, protection from, 55
Low Earth orbit, 16
Lunar bases:
    benefits of, 18, 22
    construction of, 46–47, 49
    energy sources for, 26, 29
    exercise facilities on, 42, 43
    food on, 39–40
    health care on, 40, 43
    mining operations on, 26,
        27, 50, 51, 52–53, 54–55
    motion sickness on, 30
    opposition to, 55
    programs and planning for,
        15

Lunar Bases (*continued*)
    protection of, 35, 55
    tourism to, 15
    water sources for, 26
    weightlessness on, 29–30,
        31
    workers on, 44, 45, 46
Lunar ferry, 12, 13
Lunar houses:
    artificial gravity in, 38
    constructed from external
        fuel tank, 39
    interconnection of, 38
    lava tunnel as, 36–37
    prefabricated, 35
    protective shield for, 35, 38,
        55
    size of, 38–39
    underground, 38

Manipulators, electromechanical,
    47, 48, 49
Mars, 15, 17, 20–21
Mass driver, 54, 55
Medical researchers, 44
Melters, solar-powered, 54
Metabolism, 26
Meteorite, 34
Meteorologists, 44
Mining equipment, 50, 54
Mir, 33
Moon:
    environment on, 23–24
    natural resources on, 50,
        52–53, 54, 56

Moon (*continued*)
    rocks from, 24–26
    temperature on, 25–26
    See also Lunar bases; Lunar
      houses
Motion sickness, 30
Mountains, 23
Muses-A, 15

National Aeronautics and Space
  Administration (NASA), 35, 39
National Commission on Space,
  15
Nitrogen, 26
Nuclear stations, 28, 29

Observatories, 18, 19
Oxygen production, 10–11, 26,
  54

Payloads, 54
Phobos, 17, 20–21
Propellant dump, 13

Rescue spaceship, 40, 41
Robots, 17, 46, 54
Rocks, lunar, 24–26

Satellites:
    astronomy, 18
    repairing, 18
    solar-powered, 26, 29, 46

Scientists, 44, 51
Seismologists, 44
Silicon, 54
Simulating, 29
Society Expeditions, 15
Soil, lunar:
    as building material, 38,
      55
    gathering/processing, 54
    as natural resource, 50,
      52–53
Solar energy, 26, 29, 54
Soviet Union:
    cosmonauts, 15, 30, 33
    lunar mission of, 15
Space center, 12, 13
Space suit, 10, 47
Space tug, 46
Surgery, 40

Telescopes, 18, 19
Temperature, 25–26

Van Allen, James, 55

Water, 26
Weightlessness, 29–30,
  31

Young, John, 55

Zero gravity, 12